Hugo's Simplified System

Italian Verbs Simplified

Hugo's Language Books Ltd, London

This enlarged edition
© 1986 Hugo's Language Books Ltd
All rights reserved
ISBN 0 85285 096 4

Original edition compiled by

L. Panizza Jackson M.A.
and
dott. **A. M. Saporito Minghetti**

Set in 9/11pt Linotron 202 Times by
Tek Translation Ltd., London W12 8LH
Printed and bound in Great Britain by
Anchor Brendon Ltd., Tiptree, Essex

Preface

The greater part of this book is for reference only, and in common with others in our 'Simplified' and 'Three Months' series its object is to save the student's time by giving no rules other than those actually necessary.

The models of regular verbs (pages 14–17) should be learned first of all. When the regular verbs have been mastered, the irregular ones should present little difficulty.

No English for the subjunctive should be learned. The translation usually given—'that I may speak' or 'might speak'—is most misleading and often absolutely wrong. The only safe way is to learn when to use it.

Fuller conjugations of the compound tenses, and of the negative and interrogative forms, are omitted because they require no learning whatever. Some publications treat them exhaustively and only succeed in disheartening the student. Their formation is precisely the same throughout every verb in the language—learn one and you have learned them all.

Where necessary, we show which syllable takes the stress by placing a dot under the vowel concerned (as in pạrlano, *they speak*). This dot is, of course, not used in written Italian.

We believe that this book will be found a great help to the beginner who has not yet mastered Italian verbs, and an invaluable reference book for the more advanced student.

Contents

Structure of a verb 5

Subject pronouns 7

Italian conjugations 9

Infinitive, gerund and participle 12

Complete regular conjugations 14
'Parlare', 'temere'
'Dormire', 'capire'

Auxiliary verbs 'essere' and 'avere' 18
Complete conjugations

Formation and use of tenses 20
Present, imperfect, past definite, future, conditional, present/imperfect subjunctive, imperative

Compound tenses 26

When to use 'essere' 28

Subject/object agreement with past participles 30

The passive voice 31

Impersonal verbs 31

Reflexive verbs 34

'Dovere' and 'potere' as auxiliaries 36

Negative and interrogative forms 38

Irregular verbs 39
Tables showing irregularities
Complete alphabetical list of irregular verbs 89

A model English verb 95

Structure of a verb

The verb is the most important part of speech in any language, and should therefore be learned as thoroughly as possible. If you are a little uncertain about its general structure, the following notes may help to refresh your memory. See also pages 95–96 for a model English verb, partially conjugated.

In this book you will find tables showing the conjugations of Italian verbs. To conjugate a verb means to show all its different forms.

Verbs can be *transitive* or *intransitive*. Transitive verbs are so called because they transmit the action from the subject to the object. Intransitive verbs convey a complete meaning without the addition of an object. *Roger hit* conveys no special meaning, but *Roger* (subject) *hit* (verb) *the car* (object) is a complete sentence. The verb *hit* is transitive. *It rains, she smiles*, make sense without the addition of an object. The verbs *rains, smiles* are intransitive.

Many verbs can be transitive or intransitive depending on their use in a particular sentence. *I'm singing* is intransitive, but *I'm singing a song* is transitive. *He grew* is intransitive, *he grew a beard*, transitive.

Verbs consist of two *voices* (active and passive), four *moods* (infinitive, indicative, subjunctive and imperative), three principal *tenses* (present, past, future), two *numbers* (singular and plural), and three *persons* in each number (1st, 2nd and 3rd).

In the active voice, the subject of the verb is the doer of the action expressed: *Susan* (subject) *is eating* (verb). The active voice often expresses a state or condition: *the river flows, the children rest.* In the passive voice, the subject receives the action expressed: *The apple was eaten, the car was hit.*

Of the four moods, the *infinitive* is the word given in the dictionary (*dimostrare*, to show; *rimanere*, to stay) and is in effect the name of the verb. It expresses the action itself, without any reference to time or to the person doing the action. In Italian, the infinitive is called an indefinite mood, and is discussed together with participles and gerunds. This book will discuss infinitives, participles and gerunds together as well.

The *indicative* is by far the most used mood. It indicates or expresses a thing as a fact in present, past, or future time, rather than as a wish or a possibility.

The *subjunctive* has almost completely disappeared in English, but is still vigorous in Italian. It expresses wish or possibility (*Se fossi ricca!* If I were rich!); it is nearly always found in dependent sentences introduced by a form of *che*. For a full explanation, see our 'Italian in Three Months'.

The *imperative* mood is used for giving an order or command (*Si accomodi*, Sit down! *Va' via*, Go away!). The imperative has only one tense, the present, and only two persons, the 2nd (*you*) person singular and plural. However, expressions such as *Andiamo!* (Let's go!) and *Mangiamo!* (Let's eat!) are also classified as imperative.

If a verb has only one person or thing as its subject, its *number* is *singular*. If it has more than one person or thing as its subject, its number is *plural*. *I'm studying* is singular; *They're fighting* is plural. The 1st person is identified by the personal pronouns *I* and *we*; the 2nd person by *you* (singular and plural), and the 3rd person by *he, she, it,* and *they*. Tenses are always arranged in the following order:

1st person singular	I paint
2nd person singular	you paint
3rd person singular	he, she, it paints
1st person plural	we paint
2nd person plural	you paint
3rd person plural	they paint

Subject pronouns

Where in English personal subject pronouns such as *I, you, he, she, we, they* are necessary with verbs, in Italian they are rarely needed as the ending of the verb gives information about the person: *Compro,* I buy; *compr**ano**,* they buy.

A useful rule for Italian is to avoid using *io, tu, lui, lei, noi, voi, loro* unless you have a particular reason for adding them, such as to avoid ambiguity or a desire for emphasis.

Ambiguity normally arises in the 3rd persons singular and plural. *Compr**a*** can mean *he buys, she buys,* or *you buy*. In the 3rd person in Italian, you also have a wide choice of subject pronouns and the greatest difficulty in deciding upon which one to use.

In every conversation and letter-writing to friends, use *lui* and *lei* for *he* and *she*. *Egli* for *he* is slightly formal, and *ella* for *she* even more so, but you will come across these forms in books as well as in newspapers and magazines, and to some extent in conversation. *Essa* for *she* is also used sometimes although this form is usually reserved for an object rather than a person. Thus

Lui va in montagna quest' estate
He's going to the mountains this summer

Lei va al mare
She's going to the sea

In everyday conversation and letter-writing to friends, use *loro* for *they*. *Essi* and *esse* are used in more formal written Italian, or to make a distinction between a masculine *they* and a feminine *they*.

Never translate *it* when it is the subject of a verb. There do exist the forms *esso* and *essa* for the masculine and feminine *it* as subject, but the safest policy is to avoid using them:

La casa è vecchia e sembra anche piccola
The house is old and it also seems small

E'una bella giornata
It's a lovely day

In English, whether you address the Queen or a close relative, the correct form is *you*. In Italian, on the contrary, there are two forms of address, a familiar form and a polite one. With friends, relatives, colleagues, and children, use the familiar *tu* and *voi*.

N.B. Throughout this book, *tu* will always be translated by *you*, its modern equivalent. The 2nd person singular in English used to be *thou*. As this form is obsolete, it would be confusing to equate it with the Italian *tu*, which the student will find very much alive when he goes to Italy.

With acquaintances, elders and betters, *Lei* is used in the singular. In the plural, the corresponding form *Loro* often gives way nowadays to *voi*, which is also used extensively in addressing meetings or speaking to an audience.

With *tu* and *voi* the 2nd person singular and plural is used; with *Lei* and *Loro*, the 3rd person singular and plural is used. Consequently, the forms for *Lei* and *Loro* are exactly the same as those for *he, she, it*, and *they*. Italian subject pronouns will not be given in the tables that follow, but for your reference you will find below the corresponding forms in English and Italian for the various persons:

1st person singular	I	*io*
2nd person singular	you (familiar)	*tu*
3rd person singular	he, she it	*lui, lei*
	also you (polite)	*Lei*
1st person plural	we	*noi*
2nd person plural	you (familiar)	*voi*
3rd person plural	they	*loro, essi, esse*
	also you (polite)	*Loro*

Italian conjugations

There are three conjugations in Italian, recognized by the endings *-are, -ere, -ire* of the infinitive. The first conjugation is recognized by the ending *-are* as in *parlare* (to speak), *cambiare* (to change); the second conjugation by the ending *-ere* as in *credere* (to believe), *dividere* (to divide); the third by the ending *-ire* as in *dormire* (to sleep), *finire* (to finish). The part of the infinitive preceding the ending is called the stem. Italian verbs are conjugated by adding a variety of different endings to the stem, as you can see in the table of regular verbs, pp. 14–17.

The First Conjugation

All verbs of the 1st conjugation—and there are some six thousand—are regular with the exception of four very common ones: *andare* (to go), *dare* (to give), *fare* (to do or to make), and *stare* (to be, stay, remain or stand).

There are some minor spelling changes within certain groups of 1st conjugation verbs:

1. Verbs ending in *-care* and *-gare,* like *cercare* (to look for) and *pagare* (to pay), add *h* before endings beginning with *e* or *i* in the present and future tenses so as to preserve the same sound of the stem throughout. See the present and future tenses of *pagare* below:

Present: *pago, pag**h**i, paga, pag**h**iamo, pagate, pagano*
Future: *pag**h**erò, pag**h**erai, pag**h**erà, pag**h**eremo, pag**h**erete, pag**h**eranno*

2. Verbs ending in *-ciare* and *-giare,* like *cominciare* (to begin), and *mangiare* (to eat), drop the *i* in *-ciare* and *-giare* before endings beginning with *e* or *i* in the present and future tenses because in these circumstances the *i* is not necessary to preserve the sound of the stem. See the present and future tenses of *mangiare* that follow:

Present: *mangio, mangi, mangia, mangiamo, mangiate, mangiano*
Future: *mangerò, mangerai, mangerà, mangeremo, mangerete, mangeranno*

3. Verbs ending in *-iare* drop the *i* (before the *i* ending of the 2nd person of the present tense) if the *i* is not in the stressed syllable of the verb. Thus *studiare* becomes *stụdio, stụdi*; while *spiare* becomes *spịo, spu*.

The Second Conjugation

While in the 1st conjugation there are very few irregular verbs, in the 2nd conjugation there are very few regular ones.

There are alternative forms for the past definite of some 2nd conjugation verbs. These forms will sometimes be encountered and therefore need to be recognized, but the learner will always be correct in using the regular ones, found in the table on p. 15.

You will find below the regular and alternative forms for the verb *credere* (to believe). Note that alternative forms exist only for the 1st and 3rd persons singular and the 3rd person plural.

Regular: *credei, credesti, credé, credemmo, credeste, crederono*
Alternative: ***credetti**, credesti, **credette**, credemmo, credeste, **credettero***

In the present tense of some 2nd conjugation verbs, the pronunciation changes while the spelling of the stem and endings remains exactly the same. Thus in verbs ending in *-cere* and *-gere*, like *vincere* (to conquer), *torcere* (to twist), *leggere* (to read), and *spingere* (to push), the pronunciation changes when *o* or *a* follow the *c* or *g*. For example, look at the following present tenses of *vincere* and *leggere*:

*vin**co**, vinci, vince, vinciamo, vincete, vin**cono***
*leg**go**, leggi, legge, leggiamo, leggete, leg**gono***

The Third Conjugation

Most verbs of the 3rd conjugation insert *-isc-* between the stem and the endings of the present tense of the indicative and subjunctive.

The following verbs and their compounds are conjugated like *partire* (to leave) and **never** insert *-isc-*:

aprire	to open	*partire*	to leave
avvertire	to warn	*pentirsi*	to repent
bollire	to boil	*seguire*	to follow
convertire	to convert	*servire*	to serve
coprire	to cover	*soffrire*	to suffer
cucire	to sew	*sortire*	to go out
divertire	to entertain	*venire*	to come
divertirsi	to enjoy oneself	*vestirsi*	to get dressed
fuggire	to flee	*udire*	to hear
morire	to die	*uscire*	to go out

There are a few verbs which may be conjugated with or without *-isc-*. The most common are:

mentire (to lie); *mento* or *mentisco*
inghiottire (to swallow); *inghiotto* or *inghiottisco*
applaudire (to applaud); *applaudo* or *applaudisco*

If in doubt, consult a modern Italian dictionary.

Infinitive, Gerund & Participle

The infinitive

The infinitive must often be used in Italian where in English you would have a choice between an infinitive or a gerund. The infinitive is also used where in English a gerund would have to be used as, for example, after a preposition:

Mi piace ***nuotare***
I like to swim *or* I like swimming

Per me, il ***cucinare*** *è un divertimento*
For me, cooking is a lot of fun

Quest'olio si usa per ***cucinare***
This oil is used for cooking

Ci vuole pazienza nel ***guidare***
One needs patience in driving

The gerund

The gerund in Italian is formed by adding *-ando* or *-endo* to the stem: *parlare—parlando, credere—credendo, dormire—dormendo.* It corresponds to the *-ing* form in English: *speaking, believing, sleeping.* The gerund in Italian is seldom used. You will come across it in the present and imperfect progressive tenses (see under heading Idiomatic Tenses) and in a few other cases. When it is used on its own as a noun it must be translated into English by a phrase or clause:

Sbagliando *si impara*
One learns by making mistakes

Fumando *troppo, ci si rovina la salute*
When you smoke too much, you ruin your health

The participle

The present participle in Italian, formed by adding *-ante* or *-ente* to the stem (*parlare—parlante, credere—credente, dormire—dormente*), also corresponds to the *-ing* form in English. This form, however, is not used as a verb any more but rather as an adjective or a noun as the examples below will show:

un ***brillante*** *successo*	a brilliant success
una commedia ***divertente***	an amusing comedy
un uomo ***importante***	an important man
un ***commandante***	a commander
un ***rappresentante***	a representative
un ***combattente***	a combatant
un ***insegnante***	a teacher
un ***assistente***	an assistant

See also p. 30 for more concerning the past participle.

Complete regular conjugations

INFINITIVE:	**to speak parl*ąre***	**to fear tem*ęre***
GERUND:	speaking parl*ąndo*	fearing tem*ęndo*
PAST PARTICIPLE:	spoken parl*ąto*	feared tem*ęto*
PRESENT INDICATIVE:	I speak, etc.	I fear, etc.
	pąrl*o*	tęm*o*
	pąrl*i*	tęm*i*
	pąrl*a*	tęm*e*
	parl*iąmo*	tem*iąmo*
	parl*ąte*	tem*ęte*
	pąrl*ano*	tęm*ono*
FUTURE:	I shall speak, etc.	I shall fear, etc.
	parl*erò*	tem*erò*
	parl*erąi*	tem*erąi*
	parl*erà*	tem*erà*
	parl*eręmo*	tem*eręmo*
	parl*eręte*	tem*eręte*
	parl*erąnno*	tem*erąnno*
CONDITIONAL:	I should speak, etc.	I should fear, etc.
	parl*eręi*	tem*eręi*
	parl*eręsti*	tem*eręsti*
	parl*erębbe*	tem*erębbe*
	parl*eręmmo*	tem*eręmmo*
	parl*eręste*	tem*eręste*
	parl*erębbero*	tem*erębbero*
IMPERFECT:	I was speaking, etc.	I was fearing, etc.
	parl*ąvo*	tem*ęvo*
	parl*ąvi*	tem*ęvi*
	parl*ąva*	tem*ęva*
	parl*avąmo*	tem*evąmo*
	parl*avąte*	tem*evąte*
	parl*ąvano*	tem*ęvano*

PAST DEFINITE:	I spoke, etc.	I feared, etc.
	parl*ąi*	tem*ęi* (tem*ętti*)
	parl*ąsti*	tem*ęsti*
	parl*ò*	tem*é* (tem*ętte*)
	parl*ąmmo*	tem*ęmmo*
	parl*ąste*	tem*ęste*
	parl*ąrono*	tem*ęrono* (tem*ęttero*)

PRESENT SUBJUNCTIVE: (No English equivalent is possible)

pąrl*i*	tęm*a*
pąrl*i*	tęm*a*
pąrl*i*	tęm*a*
parl*iąmo*	tem*iąmo*
parl*iąte*	tem*iąte*
pąrl*ino*	tęm*ano*

IMPERFECT SUBJUNCTIVE: (No English equivalent is possible)

parl*ąssi*	tem*ęssi*
parl*ąssi*	tem*ęssi*
parl*ąsse*	tem*ęsse*
parl*ąssimo*	tem*ęssimo*
parl*ąste*	tem*ęste*
parl*ąssero*	tem*ęssero*

IMPERATIVE: (See page 24 for English equivalents)

Familiar:	pąrl*a* (tu)	tęm*i* (tu)
	parl*iąmo* (noi)	tem*iąmo* (noi)
	parl*ąte* (voi)	tem*ęte* (voi)
	pąrl*i* (Lei)	tęm*a* (Lei)
Polite:	pąrl*ino* (Loro)	tęm*ano* (Loro)

INFINITIVE:	**to sleep dormi*ṛe***	**to understand capi*ṛe***
GERUND:	sleeping dormi*ṛe*	understanding capi*ṛe*
PAST PARTICIPLE:	slept dormi*to*	understood capi*to*
PRESENT INDICATIVE:	I sleep, etc. dormo dormi dorme dormi*ąmo* dormi*te* dormo*no*	I understand, etc. capi*sco* capi*sci* capi*sce* capi*ąmo* capi*te* capi*scono*
FUTURE:	I shall sleep, etc. dormi*rò* dormi*rąi* dormi*rà* dormi*rẹmo* dormi*rẹte* dormi*rąnno*	I shall understand, etc. capi*rò* capi*rąi* capi*rà* capi*rẹmo* capi*rẹte* capi*rąnno*
CONDITIONAL:	I should sleep, etc. dormi*rẹi* dormi*rẹsti* dormi*rẹbbe* dormi*rẹmmo* dormi*rẹste* dormi*rẹbbero*	I should understand, etc. capi*rẹi* capi*rẹsti* capi*rẹbbe* capi*rẹmmo* capi*rẹste* capi*rẹbbero*
IMPERFECT:	I was sleeping, etc. dormi*vo* dormi*vi* dormi*va* dormi*vąmo* dormi*vąte* dormi*vano*	I was understanding, etc. capi*vo* capi*vi* capi*va* capi*vąmo* capi*vąte* capi*vano*

PAST DEFINITE:	I slept, etc.	I understood, etc.
	dormi*i*	capi*i*
	dormi*sti*	capi*sti*
	dormì	capì
	dormi*mmo*	capi*mmo*
	dormi*ste*	capi*ste*
	dormi*rono*	capi*rono*

PRESENT SUBJUNCTIVE: (No English equivalent is possible)

dormi*a*	capi*sca*
dormi*a*	capi*sca*
dormi*a*	capi*sca*
dormi*amo*	capi*amo*
dormi*ate*	capi*ate*
dormi*ano*	capi*scano*

IMPERFECT SUBJUNCTIVE: (No English equivalent is possible)

dormi*ssi*	capi*ssi*
dormi*ssi*	capi*ssi*
dormi*sse*	capi*sse*
dormi*ssimo*	capi*ssimo*
dormi*ste*	capi*ste*
dormi*ssero*	capi*ssero*

IMPERATIVE: (See page 24 for English equivalents)

Familiar:	dormi (tu)	capi*sci* (tu)
	dormi*amo* (noi)	capi*amo* (noi)
	dormi*te* (voi)	capi*te* (voi)
Polite:	dormi*a* (Lei)	capi*sca* (Lei)
	dormi*ano* (Loro)	capi*scano* (Loro)

Complete auxiliary conjugations

INFINITIVE:	**to be ẹssere**	**to have avẹre**
GERUND:	being essẹndo	having avẹndo
PAST PARTICIPLE:	been stạto	had avụto
PRESENT INDICATIVE:	I am, etc. sọno sẹi è siạmo sięte sọno	I have, etc. ho hại ha abbiạmo avęte hạnno
FUTURE:	I shall be, etc. sarò sarại sarà sarẹmo sarẹte sarạnno	I shall have, etc. avrò avrại avrà avrẹmo avrẹte avrạnno
CONDITIONAL:	I should be, etc. sarẹi sarẹsti sarębbe sarẹmmo sarẹste sarębbero	I should have, etc. avrẹi avrẹsti avrębbe avrẹmmo avrẹste avrębbero
IMPERFECT:	I was, etc. ẹro ẹri ẹra eravạmo eravạte ẹrano	I had, etc. avẹvo avẹvi avẹva avevạmo avevạte avẹvano

PAST DEFINITE:	I was, etc.	I had, etc.
	fụi	ębbi
	fǫsti	avęsti
	fu	ębbe
	fụmmo	avęmmo
	fǫste	avęste
	fụrono	ębbero

PRESENT SUBJUNCTIVE: (No English equivalent is possible)

	sịa	ąbbia
	sịa	ąbbia
	sịa	ąbbia
	siąmo	abbiąmo
	siąte	abbiąte
	sịano	ąbbiano

IMPERFECT SUBJUNCTIVE: (No English equivalent is possible)

	fǫssi	avęssi
	fǫssi	avęssi
	fǫsse	avęsse
	fǫssimo	avęssimo
	fǫste	avęste
	fǫssero	avęssero

IMPERATIVE: (See page 24 for English equivalents)

Familiar:	sịi (tu)	ąbbi (tu)
	siąmo (noi)	abbiąmo (noi)
	siąe (voi)	abbiąte (voi)
Polite:	sịa (Lei)	ąbbia (Lei)
	sịano (Loro)	ąbbiano (Loro)

Formation & use of tenses

Present

Note that the endings for the 1st person singular (*parl**o**, cred**o**, dorm**o**, finisc**o***), the 2nd person singular (*parl**i**, cred**i**, dorm**i**, finisc**i***), and the 1st person plural (*parl**iamo**, cred**iamo**, dorm**iamo**, fin**iamo***) are the same for all conjugationes.

The stress for the 3rd person plural falls on the same syllable as the stress for the 1st, 2nd and 3rd persons singular as follows:

desịdero	*desịderi*	*desịdera*	—	—	*desịderano*
ạbito	*ạbiti*	*ạbita*	—	—	*ạbitano*

A present tense verb in Italian such as *parlo* expresses the English *I speak, I am speaking, I do speak.* There is an Italian present progressive, *sto parlando,* I am speaking, but it is used far less than the English. (For its specific uses, see section on idiomatic tenses.) Avoid this tense and use the ordinary present tense unless you are quite sure of what you are saying.

In Italian there are no auxiliary verbs for asking questions or expressing negation. (See section on the negative form and the interrogative form.)

The English present perfect progressive used with expressions of time is translated into Italian by the present. Thus:

How long have you been living here?
*Da quanto tempo **abiti** qui?*

I have been living in London for two years
***Abito** a Londra da due anni*

Imperfect

This is the easiest Italian tense to form—but not the easiest to use! The endings are the same for all conjugations; the only change is in the characteristic vowel of the infinitive: *parl**a**re—parl**a**vo* etc., *cred**e**re—cred**e**vo* etc., *dorm**i**re—dorm**i**vo* etc., fin**i**re—fin**i**vo* etc.

The imperfect tense is easily recognized by the presence of the letter *v* in all persons singular and plural for all conjugations. This letter is not used as a regular part of an ending in any other tense.

The imperfect Italian verb *parlavo* expresses the English *I was speaking, I used to speak*, as well as *I spoke.* This tense is used whenever writing descriptive passages or whenever referring to actions repeated in the past:

A thick fog covered the valley
Una fitta nebbia **copriva** *la valle*

Every year we went to the mountains
Tutti gli anni **andavamo** *in montagna*

The imperfect is always used in Italian to refer to an action that is continuing while another takes place:

While I was reading, the telephone rang
Mentre **leggevo**, *suonò il telefono*

There is a tendency for verbs of thinking, willing, believing and feeling to use the imperfect instead of the past definite or the present perfect. Thus:

I wanted to leave
***Volevo** andar via*

I thought I'd take the tram
***Pensavo** di prendere il tram*

I had a headache. I felt ill
***Avevo** mal di testa. Mi **sentivo** male*

Past Definite

The endings of this tense are very similar in all three conjugations. In all forms but one (*parlò*), the endings are introduced by the characteristic vowel of the infinitive. The stress always falls on this characteristic vowel, never on the stem. An accent is generally used in the 3rd person singular (parlò, credé, dormì, finì).

The above holds true for regular verbs only. Unfortunately, this tense is more irregular than any other, but even so, there is a pattern formed within the irregular past definite of 2nd conjugation *-ere* verbs. The 1st and 3rd person singular and the 3rd person plural are always the irregular forms, and the other persons are always regular. This rule is very important to remember as irregular *-ere* verbs are very numerous. See below the regular and irregular forms of the past definite of *rispondere* (to answer), and *piacere* (to be pleasing):

rispondere		*piacere*	
REGULAR FORMS	IRREGULAR FORMS	REGULAR FORMS	IRREGULAR FORMS
—	risposi	—	piacqui
rispondesti	—	piacesti	—
—	rispose	—	piacque
rispondemmo	—	piacemmo	—
rispondeste	—	piaceste	—
—	risposero	—	piacquero

In Italian, this tense need hardly ever be used in conversation. In Northern Italy, in fact, Italians tend to use the present perfect instead. To express *I spoke to him*, they would say *gli ho parlato* rather than *gli parlai*. In Southern Italy, on the other hand, this tense is still used in conversation. It is certainly used in written Italian whether of a journalistic or literary bent.

Future and Conditional

For both future and conditional tenses, the entire infinitive less the final vowel is used as a stem to which endings are added. In the 1st conjugation, however, the characteristic vowel *a* changes to *e*: *abit**a**re—abit**e**rò, abit**e**rei,* etc. In these two tenses, the stress always falls on the endings, never on the stem.

The 3rd person singular and plural of the conditional are easily recognized by *-bb-*:

*abitere**bbe**, abitere**bb**ero*; finire***bbe, finirebb**ero*.

The endings of the familiar forms of the conditional are deceptively similar to the past definite; note carefully the difference between *parlasti—parlaste* of the past definite and *parleresti—parlereste* of the conditional; between *credesti—credeste* and *credesti—credereste*; *dormisti—dormiste* and *dormiresti—dormireste*. dereste

The future and conditional are employed in Italian as in English. *Partirò domani* can be expressed in English as *I'll leave tomorrow* or *I'll be leaving tomorrow*; *Partirei domani* can be expressed *I'd leave tomorrow* or *I'd be leaving tomorrow*.

The conditional of *potere* (*potrei, potresti,* etc.) expresses the English *could*; and the conditional of *dovere* (*dovrei, dovresti,* etc.) the English *should* = *ought to*. (For more on *could* and *should,* see section on 'dovere' and 'potere' as auxiliary verbs.)

Present and Imperfect Subjunctive

For learning purposes there are only two conjugations in the present subjunctive, for the endings of the *-ere* and *-ire* verbs are alike in this tense. In the 1st conjugation, the characteristic vowel *a* changes to *i*, while in the 2nd and 3rd conjugations the characteristic *e* and *i* both change to *a*.

The imperfect subjunctive can always be recognized by *-ss-*: *parlassi, credessi, finissi.* Exceptions are the forms for the 2nd person plural *parlaste, credeste, finiste,* which are the same as the past definite.

For the use of the subjunctive, consult Hugo's 'Italian in Three Months.'

The Imperative

Strictly speaking, the imperative exists only for *tu* and *voi.* A *noi* form (*Mangiamo!* Let's eat! *Partiamo!* Let's leave!) is now classified with the imperative. The *tu, noi,* and *voi* forms make one pattern.

When *Lei* and *Loro* were introduced into Italian for formal address, the imperative for these was taken over from the 3rd persons of the present tense of the subjunctive, and constitute a second pattern. It is much easier to learn the two patterns separately.

The imperative for *tu, noi*, and *voi* is *exactly the same as the present tense.* There is only one exception to this rule: the *tu* form of a first conjugation verb such as *parlare* is *parla!*

The negative imperative for *tu* is *non* plus the infinitive: *Non fumare!* Don't smoke! *Non partire!* Don't leave! *Non piangere!* Don't cry!

There are a few irregular verbs with an irregular imperative for *tu*:

dare to give *da'*
Dammi quel bicchiere! Give me that glass!

stare to be, stay *sta'*
Sta' fermo! Keep still!

andare to go *va'*
Va' via! Go away!

fare to do, make *fa'*
Fa' presto! Hurry up!

dire to say, tell *di'*
Dimmi la verità! Tell me the truth!

You have probably noticed that in all of these very common verbs, the final *i* of the 2nd person simply drops off. When pronouns are added—there are two examples above—the beginning consonant is doubled.

Essere and *avere* also have irregular imperatives for *tu* and *voi.* See the table of auxiliary verbs.

The imperative for *Lei* and *Loro,* we repeat, is exactly the same as the 3rd persons of the present subjunctive. No more need be said.

Note that in Italian the *noi* form of the imperative is often written without an exclamation point, and can easily be confused with an ordinary present tense. *Andiamo fuori* could thus mean *We are going out* or *Let's go out!* You must judge by the context.

Compound tenses

Verbs may be compounded in Italian with *avere* or *essere*. The auxiliary *avere* is compounded with *avere,* and the auxiliary *essere* with *essere*. These two are shown in the following table, together with examples of ordinary verbs that take *avere* or *essere* when compounded.

Note that the final *e* of *avere* is often dropped in the perfect infinitive: *aver mangiato, aver parlato.*

Note also that the past participles of verbs taking *essere* must agree in number and gender with the subject: *stato* and *partito* (*below) become *stata, partita* if feminine, the plural forms being *stati, partiti* (masculine), *state, partite* (feminine).

INFINITIVE PERFECT	
to have had, spoken:	***avere*** *avuto, parlato*
to have been, left:	***essere*** *stato, partito*
GERUND PERFECT	
having had, spoken:	***avendo*** *avuto, parlato*
having been, left:	***essendo*** *stato, partito*
PERFECT	
I have had, spoken:	***ho*** *avuto, parlato*
I have been, left:	***sono*** *stato,* partito**
PLUPERFECT	
I had had, spoken:	***avevo*** *avuto, parlato*
I had been, left:	***ero*** *stato, partito*
PAST DEFINITE PERFECT	
I had had, spoken:	***ebbi*** *avuto, parlato*
I had been, left:	***fui*** *stato, partito*
FUTURE PERFECT	
I shall have had, spoken:	***avrò*** *avuto, parlato*
I shall have been, left:	***sarò*** *stato, partito*

CONDITIONAL PERFECT

I should have had spoken: ***avrei*** *avuto, parlato*
I should have been, left: ***sarei*** *stato, partito*

PERFECT SUBJUNCTIVE

abbia *avuto, parlato*
sia *stato, partito*

PLUPERFECT SUBJUNCTIVE

avessi *avuto, parlato*
fossi *stato, partito*

When to use 'essere'

1 *Essere* is used with verbs indicating motion:

andare to go
arrivare to arrive
entrare to enter
giungere to arrive
raggiungere to reach
fuggire to flee
cadere to fall down
partire to leave
ripartire to leave again
scappare to dash, escape
tornare to return
ritornare to return
venire to come
uscire to go out

Note that *salire* (to go up) and *scendere* (to go down) take *essere* when there is no object, but *avere* when there is one.

Sono salito in autobus
I got into the bus

Ho salito le scale
I went up the stairs

2 *Essere* is also used with verbs expressing an action or activity the subject undergoes:

crescere to grow
diventare, divenire to become
dimagrire to grow thin
invecchiare to grow old
nascere to be born
maturare to mature

morire to die
ringiovanire to grow young
rimanere to remain, stay

Come sei cresciuto!
How you've grown!

Sono diventati ricchi
They've become rich

Lei è nata a Roma
She was born in Rome

3 With verbs expressing chance:

accadere to happen
avvenire to happen
capitare to happen
succedere to happen
toccare (*a*) to concern
dipendere to depend

Che cosa è successo?
What happened?

Ieri me è accaduto qualcosa di strano
Yesterday, something strange happened to me

4 With all passive reflexive verbs.

Subject/Object agreement with past participles

Verbs compounded with *essere*

The past participle agrees in gender and number with the subject.

Il treno è partito/I treni sono partiti
The train has left/The trains have left

La ragazza è uscita/Le ragazze sono uscite
The girl has gone out/The girls have gone out

Verbs compounded with *avere*

The past participle agrees with a direct object pronoun placed immediately in front of the verb, if the direct object is a third person. Study the following examples:

Abbiamo portato i pacchi ad Elena
We took the parcels to Elena's
Li abbiamo portati ad Elena
We took them to Elena's

Ho comprato una macchina da cucire
I've bought a sewing machine
L'ho comprata
I've bought it

The past participle does not agree with an indirect object, but it does agree with the pronoun *ne* (of it, of them):

Quante mele hai comprato? Ne ho comprate cinque
How many apples have you bought? I've bought five (of them)

Hanno mangiato la torta? Ne hanno mangiate due fette
Have they eaten the cake? They've eaten two slices (of it)

The passive voice

The passive voice is formed with the auxiliary *essere* (to be) and the past participle. Remember that the past participle, after *essere*, must agree in gender and number with the subject.

The verb *venire* can be used in the passive as an auxiliary instead of *essere*:

Il Manzoni viene molto lodato
Manzoni is praised a great deal

Il ladro venne arrestato dai carabinieri
The thief was arrested by the police

Impersonal verbs

Impersonal verbs have no person or thing as their subject, and are used only in the third person. Some common examples (including verbs which refer to the weather) are:

piove (from *piovere*) it's raining
nevica (*nevicare*) it's snowing
grandina (*grandinare*) it's hailing
tuona (*tuonare*) it's thundering
lampeggia (*lampeggiare*) there's lightning
bisogna (*bisognare*), *occorre* (occorrere) it is necessary
capita (*capitare*), *accade* (*accadere*), *avviene* (*avvenire*) it happens
pare (*parere*), *sembra* (*sembrare*) it seems
basta (*bastare*) it is enough
conviene (*convenire*) it is convenient

Occorre far benzina
It is necessary to get petrol

Pare che sia tornato a casa
It seems he's gone home

Reflexive verbs

Reflexive verbs can hardly be said to exist as such in English, but they are very common in Italian. The student should be very careful about translating Italian reflexive verbs by an English reflexive pronoun. Some reflexive verbs in Italian have nothing whatsoever to do with reflexive pronouns: *comportarsi*, to behave; *lamentarsi*, to complain; *sentirsi*, to feel. Other reflexive verbs might possibly be translated by a reflexive pronoun in English, but would be better translated another way:

lavarsi to get washed (*rather than* to wash oneself)
vestirsi to get dressed (*rather than* to dress oneself)

Reflexive pronouns in Italian are used to express a reciprocal action:

Ci scrivevamo ogni giorno
We used to write to each other daily

I giocatori si lanciavano la palla
The players threw the ball to each other

All other compound tenses of reflexive verbs take *essere*, and the past participle agrees in gender and number with the subject.

Example of a reflexive verb

INFINITIVE: *to enjoy onself* divertịrsi

GERUND: *enjoying oneself* divertẹndosi

PRESENT INDICATIVE: *I enjoy myself, etc.*
mi divẹrto
ti divẹrti
si divẹrte
ci divertịamo
vi divertịte
si divẹrtono

FUTURE: *I shall enjoy myself* mi divertirò

CONDITIONAL: *I should enjoy myself* mi divertirẹi

IMPERFECT: *I was enjoying myself* mi divertịvo

PAST DEFINITE: *I enjoyed myself* mi divertịi

PRESENT SUBJUNCTIVE: mi divẹrta

IMPERFECT SUBJUNCTIVE: mi divertịssi

IMPERATIVE:
enjoy yourself divẹrtiti (*fam.*)
let us enjoy ourselves divertiạmoci (*fam.*)
enjoy yourselves divertịtevi (*fam.*)

enjoy yourself si divẹrta (*polite*)
enjoy yourselves si divẹrtano (*polite*)

PRESENT PERFECT: *I have enjoyed myself*
mi sono divertịto (*fem.*: divertita)
ti sei divertịto (*fem.*: divertita)
si è divertịto (*fem.*: divertita)
ci siamo divertịti (*fem.*: divertite)
vi siete divertịti (*fem.*: divertite)
si sono divertịti (*fem.*: divertite)

Idiomatic tenses

'Stare' + gerund

This construction is used in the present and imperfect, and sometimes in the future, to emphasize that a particular action is being done at a particular moment of the present, past or future. It also draws attention to the continuity of the action referred to. Although its translation corresponds to the English progressive, it is not used nearly as frequently.

Che fai in questo momento?
Non vedi, ***sto scrivendo*** *una cartolina*
What are you doing right now?
Can't you see, I'm writing a postcard

Quando Carlo tornò, ***stavo preparando*** *la cena*
When Charles came back, I was preparing the supper

'Stare per' + infinitive

Sto per *partire*
I am about to leave *or* I am just leaving

Stavo per *accendere la luce*
I was about to turn on the light *or* I was just turning on the light

'Andare a' + infinitive

Vado a *fare la spesa*
I am going to do the shopping

Andavo a *prenotare i biglietti*
I was going to book the tickets

'Avere' + 'da' + infinitive

This means *to have to*, and can be used instead of *dovere*:

Abbiamo da *fare le valigie*
We have to pack our suitcases

Ho da *dirti qualcosa*
I have to tell you something

'Andare' + past participle

This means *must be* + past participle; it can also be used instead of *dovere*:

Questa carne ***va fritta*** *presto*
This meat must be fried quickly

Questo ***va fatto*** *subito*
This must be done immediately

'Fare' + infinitive

Use this when you want to convey the meaning *to have something done*:

Faccio lavare *il pavimento*
I'm having the floor washed

Ha fatto *fare tanti vestiti*
She's had so many dresses made

Faranno pulire *tutta la casa*
They'll have the whole house cleaned

'Dovere' & 'potere' as auxiliaries

Both *dovere* and *potere* often have many ways f being translated into English, and it is even more difficult to translate the many English forms of *must* and *can* into Italian.

Dovere

1 This verb can mean 'to have to', 'must', 'to be obliged to', 'to be supposed to'. For example:

Devo scrivergli
I must write to him/I have to write to him/I'm supposed to write to him

Dovevo partire alle sei
I had to leave at six/I was supposed to leave at six

Dovrò partire la settimana prossima
I'll have to leave next week/I'll be obliged to leave next week

2 *Dovere* can also mean 'ought to' or 'should', when it is always translated by the conditional and conditional perfect:

Dovrei andare a rovarlo
I ought to go and see him/I should go and see him

Dovrebbero vendere quella casa
They ought to sell that house/They should sell that house

Sarei dovuto andare via
I ought to have gone away/I should have gone away

Avrebbero dovuto venderlo
They ought to have sold it/They should have sold it

3 *Dovere* meaning 'must be', 'must have been' (present and imperfect plus essere):

Devono essere molto ricchi
They must be very rich

Sua sorella dev'essere bella
Her sister must be beautiful

Dovevano essere ricchi
They must have been rich

Sua sorella doveva essere bella
Her sister must have been beautiful

Potere

The following examples will illustrate how this verb can be translated by 'to be able to', 'can', 'could', 'may' or 'might':

Posso?
May I come in?

Non possiamo leggerlo
We can't read it/We're not able to read it

Non potevano capire quel signore
They weren't able to understand that man/They couldn't understand that man

Non poteva rispondergli
She wasn't able to answer him/She couldn't answer him

Non potrai cantare quella canzone
You won't be able to sing that song

Potrei passare da te domani?
Could I (= would I be able to) pass by tomorrow?/Might I pass by tomorrow?

Potrebbe prestami la macchina da scrivere?
Could you (= would you be able to) lend me the typewriter?

Non potrebbe farlo
He couldn't do it/He wouldn't be able to do it

Non avrebbe potuto farlo
He couldn't have done it/He wouldn't have been able to do it

Negative & interrogative forms

Negations are made in Italian by placing *non* immediately in front of the verb. In compound tenses, the *non* is placed immediately in front of the auxiliary verb. *Do, does, did* are never translated.

Non capisco. Non hai finito?
I don't understand. Haven't you finished?

Non abbiamo sentito. Non avevano riposto
We haven't heard. They hadn't answered.

Questions

Most of the time no change in word order is made in Italian when asking a question. There is merely a change in intonation when speaking and the addition of a question mark when writing. The English *do, does, did* are never translated:

Parlano inglese?
Do they speak English?

Hai capito la domanda?
Have you understood the question?

Non esci stasera?
Aren't you going out this evening?

Sometimes questions are formed by inverting the order of the subject and predicate; it would be equally correct to keep the normal order:

I vostri amici arrivano alle otto?
or: *Arrivano alle otto i vostri amici?*
Are your friends coming at eight?

I loro bambini mangiano molto?
or: *Mangiano molto i loro bambini?*
Do their children eat a lot?

Irregular verbs

On pages 40–87 you will find a list of irregular verbs, those with similar irregularities being grouped together. This list does not include derivatives that are conjugated in exactly the same way as the root verb. Such derivatives will be found in the alphabetical list of all irregular Italian verbs on pages 89–95, with cross-reference numbers indicating the root verb. Thus, if you wish to know the conjugation of *soddisfare* or *rifare*, look it up under the root verb *fare* (number 4 on page 40).

INFINITIVE	GERUND & PAST PARTICIPLE	PRESENT	FUTURE -ò, -ai, -à, -emo, -ete, -anno	CONDITIONAL -ei, -esti, -ebbe, -emmo, -este, -ebbero
1. ***andare*** *to go*	andando andato	vado vai va andiamo andate vanno	andr-	andr-
2. ***dare*** *to give*	dando dato	do dai dà diamo date danno	dar-	dar-
3. ***stare*** *to stay*	stando stato	sto stai sta stiamo state stanno	star-	star-
4. ***fare*** *to make, do*	facendo fatto	faccio fai fa facciamo fate fanno	far-	far-
5. ***dire*** *to say, tell*	dicendo detto	dico dici dice diciamo dite dicono	dir-	dir-

IMPERFECT -o, -i, -a, -amo, -ate, -ano	PAST DEFINITE	SUBJ. PRES.	SUBJ. IMPERF. -si, -si, -se, -simo, -te, -sero
andav-	andai andasti andò andammo andaste andarono	vada vada vada andiamo andiate vadano	andas-
dav-	diedi desti diede demmo deste diedero	dia dia dia diamo diate diano	des-
stav-	stetti stesti stette stemmo steste stettero	stia stia stia stiamo stiate stiano	stes-
facev-	feci facesti fece facemmo faceste fecero	faccia faccia faccia facciamo facciate facciano	faces-
dicev-	dissi dicesti disse dicemmo diceste dissero	dica dica dica diciamo diciate dicano	dices-

INFINITIVE	GERUND & PAST PARTICIPLE	PRESENT	FUTURE -ò, -ai -à -emo, -ete, -anno	CONDITIONAL -ei, -esti, -ebbe, -emmo, -este, -ebbero
6. ***piacere*** *to like*	piacendo piaciuto	piaccio piaci piace piacciamo piacete piacciono	piacer-	piacer-
7. ***tacere*** *to keep silent*	tacendo taciuto	taccio taci tace taciamo tacete tacciono	tacer-	tacer-
8. ***giacere*** *to lie*	giacendo giaciuto	giaccio giaci giace giacciamo giacete giacciono	giacer-	giacer-
9. ***trarre*** *to draw*	traendo tratto	traggo trai trae traiamo traete traggono	trarr-	trarr-
10. ***cogliere*** *to gather*	cogliendo colto	colgo cogli coglie cogliamo cogliete colgono	coglier-	coglier-

IMPERFECT -o, -i, -a, -amo, -ate, -ano	PAST DEFINITE	SUBJ. PRES.	SUBJ. IMPERF. -si, -si, -se, -simo, -te, -sero
piacev-	piacqui piacesti piacque piacemmo piaceste piacquero	piaccia piaccia piaccia piacciamo piacciate piacciano	piaces-
tacev-	tacqui tacesti tacque tacemmo taceste tacquero	taccia taccia taccia tacciamo tacciate tacciano	taces-
giacev-	giacqui giacesti giacque giacemmo giaceste giacquero	giaccia giaccia giaccia giacciamo giacciate giacciano	giaces-
traev-	trassi tracsti trasse traemmo traeste trassero	tragga tragga tragga traiamo traiate traggano	traes-
cogliev-	colsi cogliesti colse cogliemmo coglieste colsero	colga colga colga cogliamo cogliate colgano	coglies-

INFINITIVE	GERUND & PAST PARTICIPLE	PRESENT	FUTURE -ò, -ai, -à, -emo, -ete, -anno	CONDITIONAL -ei, -esti, -ebbe, -emmo, -este, -ebbero
11. ***svellere*** *to root out*	svellendo svelto	svello svelli svelle svelliamo svellete svellono	sveller-	sveller-
12. ***spegnere*** *to put out*	spegnendo spento	spengo spegni spegne spegniamo spegnete spengono	spegner-	spegner-
13. ***rimanere*** *to remain*	rimanendo rimasto	rimango rimani rimane rimaniamo rimanete rimangono	rimarr-	rimarr-
14. ***porre*** *to put*	ponendo posto	pongo poni pone poniamo ponete pongono	porr-	porr-
15. ***valere*** *to be worth*	valendo valso	valgo vali vale valiamo valete valgono	varr-	varr-

IMPERFECT -o, -i, -a, -amo, -ate, -ano	PAST DEFINITE	SUBJ. PRES.	SUBJ. IMPERF. -si, -si, -se, -simo, -te, -sero
svellev-	svelsi svellesti svelse svellemmo svelleste svelsero	svella svella svella svelliamo svelliate svelliano	svelles-
spegnev-	spensi spegnesti spense spegnemmo spegneste spensero	spenga spenga spenga spegniamo spegniate spengano	spegnes-
rimanev-	rimasi rimanesti rimase rimanemmo rimaneste rimasero	rimanga rimanga rimanga rimaniamo rimaniate rimangano	rimanes-
ponev-	posi ponesti pose ponemmo poneste posero	ponga ponga ponga poniamo poniate pongano	pones-
valev-	valsi valesti valse valemmo valeste valsero	valga valga valga valiamo valiate valgano	vales-

INFINITIVE	GERUND & PAST PARTICIPLE	PRESENT	FUTURE -ò, -ai, -à, -emo, -ete, -anno	CONDITIONAL -ei, -esti, -ebbe, -emmo, -este, -ebbero
16. ***salire*** *to ascend*	salendo salito	salgo sali sale saliamo salite salgono	salir-	salir-
17. ***sedere*** *to sit*	sedendo seduto	siedo (seggo) siedi siede sediamo sedete siedono (seggono)	seder-	seder-
18. ***tenere*** *to hold*	tenendo tenuto	tengo tieni tiene teniamo tenete tengono	terr-	terr-
19. ***venire*** *to come*	venendo venuto	vengo vieni viene veniamo venite vengono	verr-	verr-
20. ***dolere*** *to ache*	dolendo dolto *or* doluto	dolgo duoli duole dogliamo dolete dolgono	dorr-	dorr-

IMPERFECT -o, -i, -a, -amo, -ate, -ano	PAST DEFINITE	SUBJ. PRES.	SUBJ. IMPERF. -si, -si, -se, -simo, -te, -sero
saliv-	salii salisti salì salimmo saliste salirono	salga salga salga saliamo saliate salgano	salis-
sedev-	sedei sedesti sedé (sedette) sedemmo sedeste sederono (sedettero)	sieda sieda sieda sediamo sediate siedano (seggano)	sedes-
tenev-	tenni tenesti tenne tenemmo teneste tennero	tenga tenga tenga teniamo teniate tengano	tenes-
veniv-	venni venisti venne venimmo veniste vennero	venga venga venga veniamo veniate vengano	venis-
dolev-	dolsi dolesti dolse dolemmo doleste dolsero	dolga dolga dolga dogliamo dogliate dolgano	doles-

INFINITIVE	GERUND & PAST PARTICIPLE	PRESENT	FUTURE -ò, -ai, -à, -emo, -ete, -anno	CONDITIONAL -ei, -esti, -ebbe, -emmo, -este, -ebbero
21. ***solęre*** *to be used*	solendo solito	soglio suoli suole sogliamo solete sogliono	—	—
22. ***volęre*** *to want*	volendo voluto	voglio vuoi vuole vogliamo volete vogliono	vorr-	vorr-
23. ***potęre*** *to be able, may, can*	potendo potuto	posso puoi può possiamo potete possono	potr-	potr-
24. ***nuǫcere*** *to hurt, harm*	nuocendo nociuto	nuoccio (noccio) nuoci nuoce nociamo nocete nuocciono (nocciono)	nuocer-	nuocer-
25. ***cuǫcere*** *to cook*	cuocendo cotto	cuocio cuoci cuoce cociamo cocete cuociono	cuocer-	cuocer-

IMPERFECT -o, -i, -a, -amo, -ate, -ano	PAST DEFINITE	SUBJ. PRES.	SUBJ. IMPERF. -si, -si, -se, -simo, -te, -sero
solev-	solei solesti solé solemmo soleste solerono	soglia soglia soglia sogliamo sogliate sogliano	soles-
volev-	volli volesti volle volemmo voleste vollero	voglia voglia voglia vogliamo vogliate vogliano	voles-
potev-	potei potesti poté potemmo poteste poterono	possa possa possa possiamo possiate possano	potes-
nuocev-	nocqui nocesti nocque nocemmo noceste noquero	noccia noccia noccia nocciamo nocciate nocciano	nuoces-
cuocev-	cossi cocesti cosse cocemmo coceste cossero	cuocia cuocia cuocia cociamo cociate cuociano	cuoces-

INFINITIVE	GERUND & PAST PARTICIPLE	PRESENT	FUTURE -ò, -ai, -à, -emo, -ete, -anno	CONDITIONAL -ei, -esti, -ebbe, -emmo, -este, -ebbero
26. ***muovere*** *to move*	muovendo mosso	muovo muovi muove moviamo movete muovono	muover-	muover-
27. ***scuotere*** *to shake*	scuotendo scosso	scuoto scuoti scuote scotiamo scotete scuotono	scuoter-	scuoter-
28. ***morire*** *to die*	morendo morto	muoio muori muore moriamo morite muoiono	morir- *or* morr-	morir- *or* morr-
29. ***udire*** *to hear*	udendo udito	odo odi ode udiamo udite odono	udir-	udir-
30. ***uscire*** *to go out*	uscendo uscito	esco esci esce usciamo uscite escono	uscir-	uscir-

IMPERFECT -o, -i, -a, -amo, -ate, -ano	PAST DEFINITE	SUBJ. PRES.	SUBJ. IMPERF. -si, -si, -se, -simo, -te, -sero
muovev-	mossi movesti mosse movemmo moveste mossero	muova muova muova muoviamo muoviate muovano	muoves-
scuotev-	scossi scotesti scosse scotemmo scoteste scossero	scuota scuota scuota scuotiamo scuotiate scuotano	scuotes-
moriv-	morii moristi morì morimmo moriste morirono	muoia muoia muoia muoiamo muoiate muoiano	moris-
udiv-	udii udisti udì udimmo udiste udirono	oda oda oda udiamo udiate odano	udis-
usciv-	uscii uscisti uscì uscimmo usciste uscirono	esca esca esca usciamo usciate escano	uscis-

INFINITIVE	GERUND & PAST PARTICIPLE	PRESENT	FUTURE -ò, -ai, -à, -emo, -ete, -anno	CONDITIONAL -ei, -esti, -ebbe, -emmo, -este, -ebbero
31. ***dovęre*** *to have to, must*	dovendo dovuto	devo (debbo) devi deve dobbiamo dovete devono (debbono)	dovr-	dovr-
32. ***parę̨re*** *to seem*	parendo parso	paio pari pare paiamo parete paiono	parr-	parr-
33. ***apparire*** *to appear*	apparendo apparso	appaio (apparisco) appari (apparisci) appare (apparisce) appariamo apparite appaiono (appariscono)	apparir-	apparir-

IMPERFECT -o, -i, -a, -amo, -ate, -ano	PAST DEFINITE	SUBJ. PRES.	SUBJ. IMPERF. -si, -si, -se, -simo, -te, -sero
dovev-	dovei (dovetti) dovesti dové (dovette) dovemmo doveste doverono (dovettero)	debba (deva) debba (deva) debba (deva) dobbiamo dobbiate debbano (devano)	doves-
parev-	parvi paresti parve paremmo pareste parvero	paia paia paia paiamo paiate paiano	parcs-
appariv-	apparvi apparisti apparve apparimmo appariste apparvero	apparisca apparisca apparisca appariamo appariate appariscano	apparis-

INFINITIVE	GERUND & PAST PARTICIPLE	PRESENT -o, -i, -e, -iamo, -ete, -ono	FUTURE -ò, -ai, -à, -emo, -ete, -anno	CONDITIONAL -ei, -esti, -ebbe, -emmo, -este, -ebbero
34. ***persuadere*** *to persuade*	persuadendo persuaso	persuad-	persuader-	persuader-
35. ***evadere*** *to evade*	evadendo evaso	evad-	evader-	evader-
36. ***radere*** *to shave*	radendo raso	rad-	rader-	rader-
37. ***ledere*** *to hurt, offend*	ledendo leso	led-	leder-	leder-
38. ***elidere*** *to elide*	elidendo eliso	elid-	elider-	elider-
39. ***chiedere*** *to ask*	chiedendo chiesto	chied-	chieder-	chieder-
40. ***conquidere*** *to win*	conquidendo conquiso	conquid-	conquider-	conquider-
41. ***decidere*** *to decide*	decidendo deciso	decid-	decider-	decider-
42. ***uccidere*** *to kill*	uccidendo ucciso	uccid-	uccider-	uccider-
43. ***ridere*** *to laugh*	ridendo riso	rid-	rider-	rider-
44. ***assidersi*** *to sit*	assidendosi assiso	mi assid-	mi assider-	mi assider-

IMPERFECT -o, -i, -a, -amo, -ate, -ano	PAST DEFINITE -si, -desti, -se, -demmo, -desto, -sero	SUBJ. PRES. -a, -a, -a, -iamo, -iate, -ano	SUBJ. IMPERF. -essi, -essi, -esse, -essimo, -este, -essero
persuadev-	persua-	persuad-	persuad-
evadev-	eva-	evad-	evad-
radev-	ra-	rad-	rad-
ledev-	le-	led-	led-
elidev-	eli-	elid-	elid-
chiedev-	chie-	chied-	chied-
conquidev-	conqui-	conquid-	conquid-
decidev-	deci-	decid-	decid-
uccidev-	ucci-	uccid-	uccid-
ridev-	ri-	rid-	rid-
mi assidev-	mi assi-	mi assid-	mi assid-

INFINITIVE	GERUND & PAST PARTICIPLE	PRESENT -o, -i, -e, -iamo, -ete, -ono	FUTURE -ò, -ai, -à, -emo, -ete, -anno	CONDITIONAL -ei, -esti, -ebbe, -emmo, -este, -ebbero
45. ***divịdere*** *to divide*	dividendo diviso	divid-	divider-	divider-
46. ***intrịdere*** *to temper*	intridendo intriso	intrid-	intrider-	intrider-
47. ***rọdere*** *to gnaw*	rodendo roso	rod-	roder-	roder-
48. ***esplọdere*** *to explode*	esplodendo esploso	esplod-	esploder-	esploder-
49. ***chiụdere*** *to close*	chiudendo chiuso	chiud-	chiuder-	chiuder-
50. ***acclụdere*** *to enclose*	accludendo accluso	acclud-	accluder-	accluder-
51. ***allụdere*** *to allude*	alludendo alluso	allud-	alluder-	alluder-
52. intrụ***dere*** *to intrude*	intrudendo intruso	intrud-	intruder-	intruder-
53. ***spạndere*** *to spill*	spandendo spanto	spand-	spander-	spander-

IMPERFECT -o, -i, -a, -amo, -ate, -ano	PAST DEFINITE -si, -desti, -se, -demmo, -desto, -sero	SUBJ. PRES. -a, -a, -a, -iamo, -iate, -ano	SUBJ. IMPERF. -essi, -essi, -esse, -essimo, -este, -essero
dividev-	divi-	divid-	divid-
intridev-	intri-	intrid-	intrid-
rodev-	ro-	rod-	rod-
esplodev-	esplo-	esplod-	esplod-
chiudev-	chiu-	chiud-	chiud-
accludev-	acclu-	acclud-	acclud-
alludev-	allu-	allud-	allud-
intrudev-	intru-	intrud-	intrud-
spandev-	span-	spand-	spand-

INFINITIVE	GERUND & PAST PARTICIPLE	PRESENT -o, -i, -e, -iamo, -ete, -ono	FUTURE -ò, -ai, -à, -emo, -ete, -anno	CONDITIONAL -ei, -esti, -ebbe, -emmo, -este, -ebbero
54. ***accẹndere*** *to light*	accendendo acceso	accend-	accender-	accender-
55. ***difẹndere*** *to defend*	difendendo difeso	difend-	difender-	difender-
56. ***appẹndere*** *to hang*	appendendo appeso	append-	appender-	appender-
57. ***prẹndere*** *to take*	prendendo preso	prend-	prender-	prender-
58. ***rẹndere*** *to render*	rendendo reso	rend-	render-	render-
59. ***scẹndere*** *to descend*	scendendo sceso	scend-	scender-	scender-
60. ***tẹndere*** *to tend*	tendendo teso	tend-	tender-	tender-
61. ***rispọndere*** *to answer, reply*	rispondendo risposto	rispond-	risponder-	risponder-
62. ***nascọndere*** *to hide*	nascondendo nascosto	nascond-	nasconder-	nasconder-
63. ***fọndere*** *to melt*	fondendo fuso	fond-	fonder-	fonder-

IMPERFECT -o, -i, -a, -amo, -ate, -ano	PAST DEFINITE -si, -ndesti, -se, -ndemmo, -ndeste, -sero	SUBJ. PRES. -a, -a, -a, -iamo, -iate, -ano	SUBJ. IMPERF. -essi, -essi, -esse, -essimo, -este, -essero
accendev-	acce-	accend-	accend-
difendev-	dife-	difend-	difend-
appendev-	appe-	append-	append-
prendev-	pre-	prend-	prend-
rendev-	re-	rend-	rend-
scendev-	sce-	scend-	scend-
tendev-	te-	tend-	tend-
rispondev-	rispo-	rispond-	rispond-
nascondev-	nasco-	nascond-	nascond-
fondev-	fusi fondesti fuse fondemmo fondeste fusero	fond-	fond-

INFINITIVE	GERUND & PAST PARTICIPLE	PRESENT -o, -i, -e, -iamo, -ete, -ono	FUTURE -ò, -ai, -à, -emo, -ete, -anno	CONDITIONAL -ei, -esti, -ebbe, -emmo, -este, -ebbero
64. ***contụndere*** *to bruise*	contundendo contuso	contund-	contunder-	contunder-
65. ***ạrdere*** *to burn*	ardendo arso	ard-	arder-	arder-
66. ***pẹrdere*** *to lose*	perdendo perso	perd-	perder-	perder-
67. ***mọdere*** *to bite*	mordendo morso	mord-	morder-	morder-
68. ***piạngere*** *to cry*	piangendo pianto	piang-	pianger-	pianger-
69. ***frạngere*** *to break*	frangendo franto	frang-	franger-	franger-
70. ***attịngere*** *to draw*	attingendo attinto	atting-	attinger-	attinger-
71. ***cịngere*** *to gird*	cingendo cinto	cing-	cinger-	cinger-
72. ***fịngere*** *to feign, pretend*	fingendo finto	fing-	finger-	finger-

IMPERFECT -o, -i, -a, -amo, -ate, -ano	PAST DEFINITE -si, -ndesti, -se, -ndemmo, -ndeste, -sero	SUBJ. PRES. -a, -a, -a, -iamo, -iate, -ano	SUBJ. IMPERF. -essi, -essi, -esse, -essimo, -este, -essero
contundev-	contu-	contund-	contund-
	-si, -ndesti, -se, -demmo, -ndeste, -sero:		
ardev-	ar-	ard-	ard-
perdev-	per-	perd-	perd-
mordev-	mor-	mord-	mord-
	-si, -gesti, -se, -gemmo, -geste, -sero:		
piangev-	pian-	piang-	piang-
frangev-	fran-	frang-	frang-
attingev-	attin-	atting-	atting-
cingev-	cing-	cing-	cing-
fingev-	fin-	fing-	fing-

INFINITIVE	GERUND & PAST PARTICIPLE	**PRESENT** **-o, -i, -e, -iamo, -ete, -ono**	**FUTURE** **-ò, -ai, -à, -emo, -ete, -anno**	CONDITIONAL -ei, -esti, -ebbe, -emmo, -este, -ebbero
73. ***dipingere*** *to paint*	dipingendo dipinto	**diping-**	**dipinger-**	dipinger-
74. ***spingere*** *to push*	spingendo spinto	**sping-**	**spinger-**	spinger-
75. ***tingere*** *to dye*	tingendo tinto	**ting-**	**tinger-**	tinger-
76. ***distinguere*** *to distinguish*	distinguendo distinto	**distingu-**	**distinguer-**	distinguer-
77. ***fungere*** *to act as*	fundendo	**fung-**	**funger-**	funger-
78. ***giungere*** *to arrive*	giungendo giunto	**giung-**	**giunger-**	**giunger-**
79. ***mungere*** *to milk*	mungendo munto	**mung-**	**munger-**	**munger-**
80. ***pungere*** *to sting*	pungendo punto	**pung-**	**punger-**	punger-
81. ***ungere*** *to grease*	ungendo unto	**ung-**	**unger-**	unger-
82. ***spargere*** *to spread, scatter*	spargendo sparso	**sparg-**	**sparger-**	sparger-

IMPERFECT -o, -i, -a, -amo, -ate, -ano	PAST DEFINITE -si, -gesti, -se, -gemmo, -geste, -sero	SUBJ. PRES. -a, -a, -a -iamo, -iate, -ano	SUBJ. IMPERF. -essi, -essi, -esse, -essimo, -este, -essero
dipingev-	dipin-	diping-	diping-
spingev-	spin-	sping-	sping-
tingev-	tin-	ting-	ting-
distinguev-	distinsti distinguesti distinse distinguemmo distingueste distinsero	distingu-	distingu-
fungev-	fun-	fung-	fung-
giungev-	giun-	giung-	giung-
mungev-	mun-	mung-	mung-
pungev-	pun-	pung-	pung-
ungev-	un-	ung-	ung-
spargev-	spar-	sparg-	sparg-

INFINITIVE	GERUND & PAST PARTICIPLE	PRESENT -o, -i, -e, -iamo, -ete, -ono	FUTURE -ò, -ai, -à, -emo, -ete, -anno	CONDITIONAL -ei, -esti, -ebbe, -emmo, -este, -ebbero
83. ***aspẹrgere*** *to sprinkle*	aspergendo asperso	asperg-	asperger-	asperger-
84. ***emẹrgere*** *to emerge*	emergendo emerso	emerg-	emerger-	emerger-
85. ***ẹrgere*** *to erect*	ergendo erto	erg-	erger-	erger-
86. ***accọrgersi*** *to realize, notice*	accorgendosi accorto	mi accorg-	mi accorger-	mi accorger-
87. ***pọrgere*** *to offer, give*	porgendo porto	porg-	porger-	porger-
88. ***sọrgere*** *to arise*	sorgendo sorto	sorg-	sorger-	sorger-
89. ***tẹrgere*** *to clean, wipe*	tergendo terso	terg-	terger-	terger-
90. ***convẹrgere*** *to converge*	convergendo converso	converg-	converger-	converger-
91. ***indụlgere*** *to indulge*	indulgendo indulto	indulg-	indulger-	indulger-
92. ***vọlgere*** *to turn*	volgendo volto	volg-	volger-	volger-

IMPERFECT -o, -i, -a, -amo, -ate, -ano	PAST DEFINITE -si, -gesti, -se, -gemmo, -geste, -sero	SUBJ. PRES. -a, -a, -a, -iamo, -iate, -ano	SUBJ. IMPERF. -essi, -essi, -esse, -essimo, -este, -essero
aspergev-	asper-	asperg-	asperg-
emergev-	emer-	emerg-	emerg-
ergev-	er-	erg-	erg-
mi accorgev-	mi accor-	mi accor-	mi accor-
porgev-	por-	porg-	porg-
sorgev-	sor-	sorg-	sorg-
tergev-	ter-	terg-	terg-
convergev-	conver-	converg-	converg-
indulgev-	indul-	indulg-	indulg-
volgev-	vol-	volg-	volg-

INFINITIVE	GERUND & PAST PARTICIPLE	PRESENT -o, -i, -e, -iamo, -ete, -ono	FUTURE -ò, -ai, -à, -emo, -ete, -anno	CONDITIONAL -ei, -esti, -ebbe, -emmo, -este, -ebbero
93. ***vịncere*** *to win*	vincendo vinto	vinc-	vincer-	vincer-
94. ***tọrcere*** *to twist*	torcendo torto	torc-	torcer-	torcer-
95. ***espẹllere*** *to expel*	espellendo espulso	espell-	espeller-	espeller-
96. ***eccẹllere*** *to excel*	eccellendo eccelso	eccell-	ecceller-	ecceller-
		-o, -i, -e, -iamo, -ite, -ono		
97. ***aprịre*** *to open*	aprendo aperto	apr-	aprir-	aprir-
98. ***coprịre*** *to cover*	coprendo coperto	copr-	coprir-	coprir-
99. ***offrịre*** *to offer*	offrendo offerto	offr-	offrir-	offrir-
100. ***soffrịre*** *to suffer*	soffrendo sofferto	soffr-	soffrir-	soffrir-

IMPERFECT -o, -i, -a, -amo, -ate, -ano	PAST DEFINITE -si, -cesti, -se, -cemmo, -ceste, -sero	SUBJ. PRES. -a, -a, -a, -iamo, -iate, -ano	SUBJ. IMPERF. -essi, -essi, -esse, -essimo, -este, -essero
vincev-	vin-	vinc-	vinc-
torcev-	tor-	torc-	torc-
espellev-	espulsi espellesti espulse espellemmo espelleste espulsero	espell-	espell-
eccellev-	eccelsi eccellesti eccelse eccellemmo eccelleste eccelsero	eccell-	eccell-
	-ii, -isti, -ì, -immo, -iste, -irono		-issi, -issi, -isse, -issimo, -iste, -issero
apriv-	apersi *or* apr-	apr-	apr-
copriv-	copersi *or* copr-	copr-	copr-
offriv-	offersi *or* offr-	offr-	offr-
soffriv-	soffersi *or* soffr-	soffr-	soffr-

INFINITIVE	GERUND & PAST PARTICIPLE	PRESENT -isco, -isci, -isce, -iamo, -ite, -iscono	FUTURE -ò, -ai, -à, -emo, -ete, -anno	CONDITIONAL -ei, -esti, -ebbe, -emmo, -este, -ebbero
101. ***proferire*** *to utter*	proferendo proferito	profer-	proferir-	proferir-
102. ***inferire*** *to infer*	inferendo inferto *or* inferito	infer-	inferir-	inferir-
		-o, -i, -e, -iamo, -ete, -ono		
103. ***correre*** *to run*	correndo corso	corr-	correr-	correr-
104. ***redimere*** *to redeem*	redimendo redento	redim-	redimer-	redimer-
105. ***assumere*** *to assume*	assumendo assunto	assum-	assumer-	assumer-

IMPERFECT -o, -i, -a, -amo, -ate, -ano	PAST DEFINITE -ii, -isti, -ì, -immo, -iste, -irono	SUBJ. PRES. -sca, -sca, -sca, -amo, -ate, -scano	SUBJ. IMPERF. -issi, -issi, -isse, -issimo, -iste, -issero
proferiv-	profersi *or* profer-	proferi-	profer-
inferiv-	infer-	inferi-	infer-
		-a, -a, -a, -iamo, -iate, -ano	-essi, -essi, -esse, -essimo, -este, -essero
correv-	corsi corrresti corse corremmo correste corsero	corr-	corr-
redimev-	redensi redimesti redense redimemmo redimeste redensero	redim-	redim-
assumev-	assunsi assumesti assunse assumemmo assumeste assunsero	assum-	assum-

INFINITIVE	GERUND & PAST PARTICIPLE	PRESENT -o, -i, -e, -iamo, -ete, -ono	FUTURE -ò, -ai, -à, -emo, -ete, -anno	CONDITIONAL -ei, -esti, -ebbe, -emmo, -este, -ebbero
106. ***mettere*** *to put*	mettendo messo	mett-	metter-	metter-
107. ***dirigere*** *to direct*	dirigendo diretto	dirig-	diriger-	diriger-
108. ***redigere*** *to write*	redigendo redatto	redig-	rediger-	rediger-
109. ***esigere*** *to exact, require*	esigendo esatto	esig-	esiger-	esiger-
110. ***affliggere*** *to afflict*	affliggendo afflitto	affligg-	affligger-	affligger-

IMPERFECT -o, -i, -a, -amo, -ate, -ano	PAST DEFINITE	SUBJ. PRES. -a, -a, -a, -iamo, -iate, -ano	SUBJ. IMPERF. -essi, -essi, -esse, -essimo, -este, -essero
mettev-	misi mettesti mise mettemmo metteste misero	mett-	mett-
dirigev-	diressi dirigesti diresse dirigemmo dirigeste diressero	dirig-	dirig-
redigev-	redassi redigesti redasse redigemmo redigeste redassero	**redig-**	redig-
esigev-	esigei (esigetti) esigesti esigé (-ette) esigemmo esigeste esigerono (esigettero)	esig-	esig-
affliggev-	afflissi affliggesti afflisse affliggemmo affliggeste afflissero	affligg-	affligg-

INFINITIVE	GERUND & PAST PARTICIPLE	PRESENT -o, -i, -e, -iamo, -ete, -ono	FUTURE -ò, -ai, -à, -emo, -ete, -anno	CONDITIONAL -ei, -esti, -ebbe, -emmo, -este, -ebbero
111. ***figgere*** *to fix*	figgendo fitto	figg-	figger-	figger-
112. ***affiggere*** *to stick*	affiggendo affisso	affigg-	affigger-	affigger-
113. ***friggere*** *to fry*	friggendo fritto	frigg-	frigger-	frigger-
114. ***leggere*** *to read*	leggendo letto	legg-	legger-	legger-
115. ***negligere*** *to neglect*	negligendo negletto	neglig-	negliger-	negliger-

IMPERFECT -o, -i, -a, -amo, -ate, -ano	PAST DEFINITE	SUBJ. PRES. -a, -a, -a, -iamo, -iate, -ano	SUBJ. IMPERF. -essi, -essi, -esse, -essimo, -este, -essero
figgev-	fissi figgesti fisse figgemmo figgeste fissero	figg-	figg-
affiggev-	affissi affiggesti affisse affiggemmo affiggeste affissero	affigg-	affig-
friggev-	frissi friggesti frisse friggemmo friggeste frissero	frigg-	frigg-
leggev-	lessi leggesti lesse leggemmo leggeste lessero	legg-	legg-
negligev-	neglessi negligesti neglesse negligemmo negligeste neglessero	neglig-	neglig-

INFINITIVE	GERUND & PAST PARTICIPLE	PRESENT -o, -i, -e, -iamo, -ete, -ono	FUTURE -ò, -ai, -à, -emo, -ete, -anno	CONDITIONAL -ei, -esti, -ebbe, -emmo, -este, -ebbero
116. ***prediligere*** *to prefer*	prediligendo prediletto	predilig-	prediliger-	prediliger-
117. ***protęggere*** *to protect*	proteggendo protetto	protegg-	protegger-	protegger-
118. ***rę̣ggere*** *to support*	reggendo retto	regg-	regger-	regger-
119. ***strụggere*** *to consume*	struggendo strutto	strugg-	strugger-	strugger-
120. ***riflęttere*** *to reflect*	riflettendo riflesso	riflett-	rifletter-	rifletter-

IMPERFECT -o, -i, -a, -amo, -ate, -ano	PAST DEFINITE	SUBJ. PRES. -a, -a, -a, -iamo, -iate, -ano	SUBJ. IMPERF. -essi, -essi, -esse, -essimo, -este, -essero
prediligev-	predilessi prediligesti predilesse prediligemmo prediligeste predilessero	predilig-	predilig-
proteggev-	protessi proteggesti protesse proteggemmo proteggeste protessero	protegg-	protegg-
reggev-	ressi reggesti resse reggemmo reggeste ressero	regg-	regg-
struggev-	strussi struggesti strusse struggemmo struggeste strussero	strugg-	strugg-
riflettev-	riflessi riflettesti riflesse riflettemmo rifletteste riflessero	riflett-	riflett-

INFINITIVE	GERUND & PAST PARTICIPLE	PRESENT -o, -i, -e, -iamo, -ete, -ono	FUTURE -ò, -ai, -à, -emo, -ete, -anno	CONDITIONAL -ei, -esti, -ebbe, -emmo, -este, -ebbero
121. ***genuflętt-tersi*** *to genuflect*	genuflett-endosi genuflesso	mi etc. genuflett-	mi etc. genufletter-	mi etc. genufletter-
122. ***annętterе*** *to annex*	annettendo annesso	annett-	annetter-	annetter-
123. ***discụtere*** *to discuss*	discutendo discusso	discut-	discuter-	discuter-
124. ***condụrre*** *to lead, drive*	conducendo condotto	conduc-	condurr-	condurr-
125. ***scrịvere*** *to write*	scrivendo scritto	scriv-	scriver-	scriver-

IMPERFECT -o, -i, -a, -amo, -ate, -ano	PAST DEFINITE	SUBJ. PRES. -a, -a, -a, -iamo, -iate, -ano	SUBJ. IMPERF. -essi, -essi, -esse, -essimo, -este, -essero
mi etc. genuflettev-	mi etc. genuflessi genuflettesti genuflesse genuflettemmo genufletteste genuflessero	mi etc. genuflett-	mi etc. genuflett-
annettev-	annessi annettesti annesse annettemmo annetteste annessero	annett-	annett-
discutev-	discussi discutesti discusse discutemmo discuteste discussero	discut-	discut-
conducev-	condussi conducesti condusse conducemmo conduceste condussero	conduc-	conduc-
scrivev-	scrissi scrivesti scrisse scrivemmo scriveste scrissero	scriv-	scriv-

INFINITIVE	GERUND & PAST PARTICIPLE	PRESENT -o, -i, -e, -iamo, -ete, -ono	FUTURE -ò, -ai, -à, -emo, -ete, -anno	CONDITIONAL -ei, -esti, -ebbe, -emmo, -este, -ebbero
126. ***vivere*** *to live*	vivendo vissuto	viv-	vivr-	vivr-
127. ***costruire*** *to build, construct*	costruendo costruito	costruisco costruisci costruisce costruiamo costruite costruiscono	costruir-	costruir-
128. ***esprimere*** *to express*	esprimendo espresso	esprim-	esprimer-	esprimer-
129. ***scindere*** *to separate*	scindendo scisso	scind-	scinder-	scinder-
130. ***concedere*** *to concede*	concedendo concesso *or* conceduto	conced-	conceder-	conceder-

IMPERFECT -o, -i, -a, -amo, -ate, -ano	PAST DEFINITE	SUBJ. PRES. -a, -a, -a, -iamo, -iate, -ano	SUBJ. IMPERF. -essi, -essi -esse, -essimo, -este, -essero
vivev-	vissi vivesti visse vivemmo viveste vissero	viv-	viv-
costruiv-	costruii (costrussi) costruisti costruì costruimmo costruiste costruirono	costruisc-	costruissi costruissi costruisse costruissimo costruiste costruissero
esprimev-	espressi esprimesti espresse esprimemmo esprimeste espressero	esprim-	esprim-
scindev-	scissi scindesti scisse scindemmo scindeste scissero	scind-	scind-
concedev-	concessi concedesti concesse concedemmo concedeste concessero	conced-	conced-

INFINITIVE	GERUND & PAST PARTICIPLE	PRESENT -o, -i, -e, -iamo, -ete, -ono	FUTURE -ò, -ai, -à, -emo, -ete, -anno	CONDITIONAL -ei, -esti, -ebbe, -emmo, -este, -ebbero
131. ***nąscere*** *to be born*	nascendo nato	nasc-	nascer-	nascer-
132. ***bere*** *to drink*	bevendo bevuto	bev-	berr-	berr-
133. ***piovere*** *to rain*	piovendo piovuto	piov-	piover-	piover-
134. ***crescere*** *to grow*	crescendo cresciuto	cresc-	crescer-	crescer-
135. ***conoscere*** *to know*	conoscendo conosciuto	conosc-	conoscer-	conoscer-

IMPERFECT -o, -i, -a, -amo, -ate, -ano	PAST DEFINITE	SUBJ. PRES. -a, -a, -a, -iamo, -iate, -ano	SUBJ. IMPERF. -essi, -essi, -esse, -essimo, -este, -essero
nascev-	nacqui nascesti nacque nascemmo nasceste nacquero	nasc-	nasc-
bevev-	bevvi bevesti bevve bevemmo beveste bevvero	bev-	bev-
piovev-	piovvi piovesti piovve piovemmo pioveste piovvero	piov-	piov-
crescev-	crebbi crescesti crebbe crescemmo cresceste crebbero	cresc-	cresc-
conoscev-	conobbi conoscesti conobbe conoscemmo conocsceste conobbero	conosc-	conosc-

INFINITIVE	GERUND & PAST PARTICIPLE	PRESENT -o, -i, -e, -iamo, -ete, -ono	FUTURE -ò, -ai, -à, -emo, -ete, -anno	CONDITIONAL -ei, -esti, -ebbe, -emmo, -este, -ebbero
136. ***cadere*** *to fall*	cadendo caduto	cad-	cadr-	cadr-
137. ***rompere*** *to break*	rompendo rotto	romp-	romper-	romper-
138. ***vedere*** *to see*	vedendo veduto	ved-	vedr-	vedr-
138b. ***assistere*** *to be present at*	assistendo assistito	assist-	assister-	assister-
139. ***devolvere*** *to devolve*	devolvendo devoluto	devolv-	devolver-	devolver-

IMPERFECT -o, -i, -a, -amo, -ate, -ano	PAST DEFINITE	SUBJ. PRES. -a, -a, -a, -iamo, -iate, -ano	SUBJ. IMPERF. -essi, -essi, -esse, -essimo, -este, -essero
cadev-	caddi cadesti cadde cademmo cadeste caddero	cad-	cad-
rompev-	ruppi rompesti ruppe rompemmo rompeste ruppero	romp-	romp-
vedev-	vidi vedesti vide vedemmo vedeste videro	ved-	ved-
assistev-	assistei assistesti assisté assistemmo assisteste assisterono		
devolvev-	devolvei (devolvetti) devolvesti devolvé dovolvemmo devolveste devolverono (devolvettero)	devolv-	devolv-

INFINITIVE	GERUND & PAST PARTICIPLE	PRESENT -o, -i, -e, -iamo, -ete, -ono	FUTURE -ò, -ai, -à, -emo, -ete, -anno	CONDITIONAL -ei, -esti -ebbe, -emmo, -este, -ebbero
140. ***seppelire*** *to bury*	seppellendo sepolto *or* seppellito	seppellisco seppellisci seppellisce seppelliamo sepellite seppelliscono	seppellir-	seppellir-
141. ***assolvere*** *to absolve*	assolvendo assolto	assolv-	assolver-	assolver-
142. ***sapere*** *to know*	sapendo saputo	so sai sa sappiamo sapete sanno	sapr-	sapr-
143. ***godere*** *to enjoy*	godendo goduto	god-	godr-	godr-
144. ***stringere*** *to draw close*	stringendo stretto	string-	stringer-	stringer-

IMPERFECT -o, -i, -a, -amo, -ate, -ano	PAST DEFINITE	SUBJ. PRES. -a, -a, -a -iamo, -iate, -ano	SUBJ. IMPERF. -essi, -essi, -esse, -essimo, -este, -essero
seppelliv-	seppellii seppellisti seppellì seppellimmo seppelliste seppellirono	seppellisc-	seppellissi seppellissi seppellisse seppellissimo seppelliste seppellissero
assolvev-	assolsi assolvesti assolvé assolvemmo assolveste assolsero	assolv-	assolv-
sapev-	seppi sapesti seppe sappemmo sapeste seppero	sappia sappia sappia sappiamo sappiate sappiano	sap-
godev-	godei (godetti) godesti godé (godette) godemmo godeste goderono (godettero)	god-	god-
stringev-	strinsi stringesti strinse stringemmo stringeste strinsero	string-	string-

INFINITIVE	GERUND & PAST PARTICIPLE	PRESENT -o, -i, -e, -iamo, -ete, -ono	FUTURE -ò, -ai, -à, -emo, -ete, -anno	CONDITIONAL -ei, -esti, -ebbe, -emmo, -este, -ebbero
145. ***rifulgere*** *to shine*	rifulgendo rifulso	rifulg-	rifulger-	rifulger-
146. ***scegliere*** *to choose*	scegliendo scelto	scelgo scegli scegle scegliamo sceglete scelgono	sceglier-	scelgier-
147. ***sciogliere*** *to melt, dissolve*	sciogliendo sciolto	sciolgo sciogli sciogle sciogliamo scioglete sciolgono	scioglier-	scioglier-
148. ***togliere*** *to take from*	togliendo tolto	tolgo togli togle togliamo toglete tolgono	toglier-	toglier-

149. ***propendere*** (*to incline*) is conjugated like a regular *-ere* verb, except in the past participle, which is propenso.

150. ***assorbire*** (*to absorb*) is conjugated like a regular *-ire* verb (present indicative: assorbo or assorbisco), but it has two past participles, assorbito and assorto.

151. ***inserire*** (*to insert*) is conjugated like a regular *-ire* verb, but it has two past participles, inserito and inserto.

IMPERFECT -o, -i, -a, -amo, -ate, -amo	PAST DEFINITE	SUBJ. PRES. -a, -a, -a, -iamo, -iate, -ano	SUBJ. IMPERF. -essi, -essi, -esse, -essimo, -este, -essero
rifulgev-	rifulsi rifulgesti rifulse rifulgemmo rifulgeste rifulsero	rifulg-	rifulg-
scegliev-	scelsi scegliesti scelse scegliemmo scelgieste scelsero	scelga scelga scelga scegliamo scegliate scelgano	scegli-
sciogliev-	sciolsi sciogliesti sciolse sciogliemmo scioglieste sciolsero	sciolga sciolga sciolga sciogliamo sciogliate sciolgano	sciogli-
togliev-	tolsi toglieste tolse togliemmo toglieste tolsero	tolga tolga tolga togliamo togliate tolgano	togli-

Defective verbs

The following verbs have only the persons and tenses given:

152. **aggradare** *to like*	Impersonal; used only in the present indicative: *mi aggrada, ti aggrada,* etc.
153. **calere** *to matter*	Obsolete, except in the present indicative: *mi cale* (it matters to me), *ti cale* (it matters to you), etc.
154. **licere** *to be permitted*	Past participle: *lecito* (permitted); present indicative: *lice* (it is permitted).
155. **molcere** *to soothe, mitigate*	Used only in poetry. Gerund: *molcendo,* present indic.: *molce* (it soothes); imperfect: *molceva.*
156. **riluсere** *to shine*	Present ind.: *riluce, rilucono;* imperfect ind.: *riluceva, rilucevano.*
157. **urgere** *to be urgent*	Impersonal. Gerund: *urgendo;* pres. ind.: *urge;* imperfect: *urgeva;* present subjunctive: *urga;* imp. subjunct.: *urgesse.*
158. **vigere** *to be in force*	Gerund: *vigendo;* pres. ind.: *vige, vigono;* imperf. ind.: *vigeva, vigevano;* imp. subjunct.: *vigesse, vigessero.*
159. **concernere** *to concern*	Impersonal. Pres. ind.: *concerne;* imperf. ind.: *concerneva;* imperf. subjunct.: *concernesse.*
160. **esimersi** *to withdraw from*	Conjugated like a regular *-ere* verb, but it has neither a past definite nor a past participle.
161. **fervere** *to be hot*	Gerund: *fervendo;* pres. ind.: *ferve;* imperf. ind.: *ferveva;* imperf. subjunct.: *fervesse.*
162. **splendere** *to shine*	A regular *-ere* verb, but it has no past participle.

Alphabetical list of irregular verbs

The number after the verb refers you to the appropriate model or root verb in the previous section.

accadęre *to happen* 136
accędere *to accede* 130
accęndere *to light, switch on* 54
acclụdere *to enclose* 50
accǫgliere *to receive, welcome* 10
accǫrgersi *to realize, notice* 86
accǫrrere *to run up to* 103
accręscere *to increase* 134
addịrsi *to suit* 5
addụrre *to convey* 124
affịggere *to stick* 112
affliggere *to afflict* 110
aggiụngere *to add* 78
aggradạre *to like* 152
allụdere *to allude* 51
ammęttere *to admit* 106
andạre *to go* 1
annęttere *to annex* 122
apparịre *to appear* 33
appartenęre *to belong* 18
appęndere *to hang* 56
appǫrre *to affix* 14
apprędere *to learn* 57
aprịre *to open* 97
ạrdere *to burn* 65
acęndere *to ascend* 59
aspęrgere *to sprinkle* 83
assalịre *to assail* 16
assịdersi *to sit* 44
assịstere *to be present* 138b
assǫlvere *to absolve* 141
assorbịre *to absorb* 150
assụmere *to assume* 105
astenęrsi *to abstain* 18
astrạrre *to abstract* 9
attęndere *to wait for* 60
attịngere *to draw up* 70
avvedęrsi *to notice* 138
avvenịre *to happen* 19
avvịncere *to tie up, unite* 93
avvǫlgere *to fold* 92
benedịre *to bless* 5
bęre *to drink* 132
cadęre *to fall* 136
calęre *to matter* 153
chiędere *to ask* 39
chiụdere *to close* 49
cịngere *to gird* 71
cǫgliere *to gather* 10
coincịdere *to coincide* 42
concęrnere *to concern* 159
conquịdere *to conquer* 40
commęttere *to commit* 106
commuǫvere *to move* 26
comparịre *to appear* 33
compiacęre *to please* 6
compiạngere *to pity* 68
compǫrre *to compose* 14
comprędere *to understand* 57
comprịmere *to compress* 128
compromęttere *compromise* 106
concędere *to concede, grant* 130

concluȩdere *or* conchiuȩdere *to conclude* 51
concǫrrere *to concur* 103
condolęrsi *to sympathize* 20
conduȩrre *to lead, drive* 124
confiȩggere *to drive in* 111
confǫndere *to confound, mix up* 63
congiuȩngere *to join* 78
connęttere *to connect* 122
conǫscere *to know* 135
consiȩstere *to consist* 138b
contęndere *to contend* 60
contenęre *to contain* 18
contǫrcere *to twist* 94
contraddiȩre *to contradict* 5
contraffąre *to counterfeit* 4
contrąrre *to contract* 9
contuȩndere *to bruise* 64
convenȩre *to agree* 19
convęrgere *to converge* 90
convȩincere *to convince* 93
coprȩire *to cover* 98
corręggere *to correct* 118
cǫrrere *to run* 103
corrispǫndere *to correspond* 1
corrǫmpere *to corrupt* 137
costrȩingere *to force* 144
costruȩire *to construct* 127
cręscere *to grow* 134
cuǫcere *to cook* 25
dąre *to give* 2
decȩidere *to decide* 41
decręscere *to decrease* 134
deduȩrre *to deduce* 124
deluȩdere *to disappoint* 51
depǫrre *to depose* 14
deprȩimere *to depress* 128
derȩidere *to deride* 43
desuȩmere *to infer* 105
descrȩivere *to describe* 125
detęrgere *to clean* 89
devǫlvere *to devolve* 139
difęndere *to defend* 55
diffǫndere *to diffuse* 63
dimęttere *to remove* 106
dipęndere *to depend* 56
dipȩingere *to paint* 73
dȩire *to say, tell* 5
dirȩigere *to direct* 107
dirǫmpere *to break* 137
discęndere *to descend* 59
dischiuȩdere *to disclose* 49
discȩogliere *to untie, dissolve* 147
discǫrrere *to talk* 103
discuȩtere *to discuss* 123
disfąre *to undo* 4
disgȩiungere *to separate* 78
disilluȩdere *to disappoint* 51
dispęrdere *to disperse* 66
dispiacęre *to displease* 6
dispǫrre *to dispose* 14
dissǫlvere *to dissolve* 141
dissuadęre *to dissuade* 34
distęndere *to stretch* 60
distȩinguere *to distinguish* 76
distǫgliere *to dissuade* 148
distǫrcere *to distort* 94
distrąrre *to distract* 9
distruȩggere *to destroy* 119
divęllere *to uproot* 11
divenȩre *to become* 19
divȩidere *to divide* 45

dolęre *to ache, hurt* 20
dovęre *to have to, must* 31
eccęllere *to excel* 96
effǫndere *to pour out* 63
elęggere *to elect* 114
elịdere *to elide* 38
elụdere *to elude* 51
emęrgere *to emerge* 84
emęttere *to emit* 106
ęrgere *to erect* 85
erịgere *to erect* 107
erǫmpere *to break* 137
esclụdere *to exclude* 51
esịgere *to exact, require* 109
esịmersi *to withdraw from* 160
espęllere *to expel* 95
esplǫdere *to explode* 48
espǫrre *to expose* 14
esprịmere *to express* 128
estęndere *to extend* 60
estịnguere *to extinguish* 76
estǫrcere *to take away, wrest* 94
estrạrre *to extract* 9
evạdere *to evade* 35
fạre *to do, make* 4
fęrvere *to be hot* 161
fịggere *to fix* 111
fịngere *to pretend* 72
fǫndere *to melt* 63
frammęttere *to interpose* 106
frạngere *to break* 69
frappǫrre *to interpose* 14
frịggere *to fry* 113
fụngere *to act as* 77
genuflęttersi *to genuflect* 121
giacęre *to lie* 8
giụngere *to arrive* 78
godęre *to enjoy* 143
illụdere *to delude, beguile* 51
immęrgere *to immerse* 84
impǫrre *to impose* 14
imprịmere *to imprint, impress* 128
incịdere *to cut* 41
inclụdere *to include* 51
incǫrrere *to incur* 103
increṣcere *to be sorry, regret* 134
incụtere *to strike* 123
indụlgere *to indulge* 91
inụrre *to induce* 124
inferịre *to infer* 102
inflịggere *to inflict* 110
infrạngere *to break* 69
infǫndere *to infuse* 63
inserịre *to insert* 151
insịstere *to insist* 138b
intęndere *to mean, intend* 60
intercędere *to intercede* 130
interdịre *to interdict* 5
interpǫrre *to interpose* 14
interrǫmpere *to interrupt* 136
intervenịre *to intervene* 19
intraprẹndere *to undertake* 57
intravedęre *to glimpse* 138
intrịdere *to temper* 46
introdụrre *to introduce* 124
intrụdere *to intrude* 52
invạdere *to invade* 35
invǫlgere *to wrap* 92
irrǫmpere *to rush upon* 136
iscrịversi *to enroll* 125
istruịre *to instruct* 127
lędere *to hurt, offend* 37
lęggere *to read* 114

lịcere *to be permitted* 154
maledịre *to curse* 5
manomẹttre *to tamper with* 106
mantenẹre *to maintain* 18
mẹttere *to put* 106
molcẹre *to soothe* 155
mọrdere *to bite* 67
morịre *to die* 28
muọvere *to move* 26
mụngere *to milk* 79
nạscere *to be born* 131
nascọndere *to hide* 62
negḷigere *to neglect* 115
nuọcere *to hurt* 24
occọrrere *to be necessary* 103
offẹndere *to offend* 55
offrịre *to offer* 99
omẹttere *to omit* 106
oppọrre *to oppose* 14
opprịmere *to oppress* 128
ottenẹre *to obtain* 18
parẹre *to seem* 32
percọrrere *to travel over* 103
percuọtere *to strike* 27
pẹrdere *to lose* 66
permẹttere *to permit* 106
persuadẹre *to persuade* 34
pervenịre *to arrive at* 19
piacẹre *to please* 6
piạngere *to cry* 68
piọvere *to rain* 133
pọrgere *to offer, give* 87
pọrre *to put* 14
pospọrre *to postpone* 14
possedẹre *to own* 17
potẹre *to be able, may, can* 23
prediḷigere *to prefer* 116
predịre *to predict* 5
prefḷggersi *to take into one's head* 112
prelụdere *to forecast, come before* 51
prẹndere *to take* 57
prepọrre *to prefer* 14
prescẹgliere *to choose from, among* 146
prescrịvere *to prescribe* 125
presiẹdere *to preside* 17
presụmere *to presume* 105
pretẹndere *to pretend* 60
prevalẹre *to prevail* 15
prevedẹre *to foresee* 138
prevenịre *to anticipate* 19
produrre *to produce* 14
proferịre *to utter* 101
profọndere *to pour out* 63
promẹttere *to promise* 106
promuọvere *to promote* 26
propẹndere *to incline* 149
propọrre *to propose* 14
prorọmpere *to burst out* 137
prosciọgliere *to free, absolve* 147
procrịvere *to proscribe* 125
protẹggere *to protect* 117
provenịre *to come from* 19
provvedẹre *to provide* 138
pụngere *to sting* 80
racchiụdere *to enclose, shut up* 49
raccọgliere *to gather* 10
rạdere *to shave* 36
raggiụngere *to reach* 78
rapprẹndere *to coagulate, thicken* 57

rattenęre *to restrain* 18
rattǫrcere *to wring* 94
ravvedęrsi *to repent* 138
ravvǫlgere *to wrap up* 92
recịdere *to cut off* 41
redịgere *to write* 108
redịmere *to redeem* 104
ręggere *to support* 119
rẹndere *to render* 58
reprịmere *to repress* 128
rescịndere *to rescind* 129
respịngere *to push back* 74
restrịngere *to restrain* 144
retrocędere *to draw back* 130
riammętere *to admit again, readmit* 106
ricadęre *to fall again* 136
richiędere *to request* 39
riconǫscere *to recognize* 135
ricoprịre *to cover again* 98
ricǫrrere *to have recourse to, apply to* 103
rịdere *to laugh* 43
ridịre *to say again* 5
ridụrre *to reduce* 124
rifąre *to do again* 4
riflętere *to reflect* 120
rifrąngere *to refract* 69
rifụlgere *to shine* 145
rilụcere *to shine* 156
rimanęre *to remain* 13
rimętere *to put back* 106
rimǫrdere *to bite again, feel remorse* 67
rimpiąngere *to regret* 68
rinąscere *to be born again* 131
rinchiụdere *to shut in* 49
rincręscere *to regret* 134
rinvenịre *to find, to recover* 19
ripercuǫtere *to strike again* 27
ripǫrre *to put again* 14
riprẹndere *to retake, recover* 57
riprodụrre *to reproduce* 124
risapęre *to know* 142
riscuǫtere *to collect, cash* 27
risǫlvere *to resolve* 141
risǫrgere *to rise up again* 88
rispǫndere *to answer, reply* 61
ristrịngere *to restrain* 144
ritenęre *to retain* 18
ritǫgliere *to recapture, retake* 148
ritrąrre *to draw* 9
riuscịre *to succeed* 30
rivedęre *to see again* 138
rivịvere *to live again* 125
rivǫlgersi *to turn to, to apply to* 92
rǫdere *to gnaw* 47
rǫmpere *to break* 137
salịre *to ascend, climb* 16
sapęre *to know* 142
scadęre *to expire, to be due* 136
scęgliere *to choose* 146
scẹndere *to descend* 59
schiụdere *to disclose* 49
scịndere *to separate* 129
sciǫgliere *to dissolve, melt* 147
scommętere *to bet* 106
scomparịre *to disappear* 33
scompǫrre *to undo* 14
sconfịggere *to defeat* 111
sconnętere *to disconnect* 122
sconvǫlgere *to overturn* 92
scoprịre *to discover* 97

scǫrgere *to perceive* 86
scǫrrere *to flow* 103
scrịvere *to write* 125
scuǫtere *to shake* 27
sedęre *to sit* 17
seppellịre *to bury* 140
smęttere *to cease* 106
smuǫvere *to move* 26
socchiụdere *to half shut* 49
soccǫrrere *to assist* 103
soddisfạre *to satisfy* 4
soffrịre *to suffer* 100
soggiụngere *to add* 78
solęre *to be accustomed* 21
sommęrgere *to submerge* 84
sopprịmere *to suppress* 128
sǫrgere *to rise* 88
sorprẹndere *to surprise* 57
sorręggere *to support* 118
sorrịdere *to smile* 43
sospẹndere *to suspend* 56
sospịngere *to push* 74
sostenęre *to support* 18
sottintẹndere *to imply* 60
sovvenịre *to remember* 19
spạndere *to spill, shed* 53
spạrgere *to spread, scatter* 82
spęgnere *to extinguish, switch off* 12
spẹndere *to spend* 56
spęrdersi *to be lost, to go astray* 66
spiacęre *to be sorry, displease* 6
spịngere *to push* 74
splẹndere *to shine* 162
spǫrgere *to lean out* 87
stạre *to stay, stand, be* 3
stẹndere *to stretch out* 60
stǫrcere *to distort, wrest* 94
strịngere *to draw close, clasp* 144
strụggere *to consume, pine away* 119
succẹdere *to happen* 130
suppǫrre *to suppose* 14
svęllere *to root out* 11
svenịre *to faint away* 19
svǫlgersi *to take place* 92
tacęre *to keep silent* 7
tẹndere *to tend, hold out* 60
tenęre *to hold, have* 18
tęrgere *to clean, wipe* 89
tịngere *to dye* 75
tǫgliere *to take from* 148
tǫrcere *to twist* 94
tradụrre *to translate* 124
trafịggere *to run through* 111
transịgere *to compromise, come to terms* 109
trạrre *to draw, pull* 9
trascǫrre *to spend (time)* 103
transcrịvere *to transcribe* 125
transmẹttere *to transmit* 106
transparịre *to show forth* 33
trattenęre *to hold back, detain* 18
travedęre *to see wrongly* 138
uccịdere *to kill* 42
udịre *to hear* 29
ụngere *to grease* 81
uscịre *to go out* 30
ụrgere *to be urgent* 157
valęre *to be worth* 15
vedęre *to see* 138
venịre *to come* 19
vịgere *to be in force* 158

vilipẹndere *to despise* 56
vịncere *to win* 93
vịvere *to live* 125
volẹre *to will* 22
vọlgere *to turn* 92

A model English verb

The following is a model of the principal tenses of an English verb. The names of the tenses are those which are generally used in the conjugation of foreign verbs. It is very important to know what English words are represented by the names *present, imperfect, future,* etc. For example, *I am calling* is just as much present as *I call,* and *I shall be calling* and *I shall call* are both future. There's no need to differentiate between the English simple present and present continuous, present perfect and simple past, and all the other variations that appear in English grammar books. But do take special notice of the auxiliaries used in the conjugation of English future and conditional.

INFINITIVE: to call

PRESENT PARTICIPLE: calling

PAST PARTICIPLE: called

PRESENT TENSE:
I call *or* I am calling
you call *or* you are calling (*singular*)
he calls *or* he is calling
we call *or* we are calling
you call *or* you are calling (*plural*)
they call *or* they are calling

IMPERFECT OR PAST:
I called *or* I was calling
you called *or* you were calling
he called *or* he was calling

we called *or* we were calling
you called *or* you were calling
they called *or* they were calling

FUTURE:
I shall call *or* I shall be calling
you will call *or* you will be calling
he will call *or* he will be calling
we shall call *or* we shall be calling
you will call *or* you will be calling
they will call *or* they will be calling

CONDITIONAL:
I should call *or* I should be calling
you would call *or* you would be calling
he would call *or* he would be calling
we shall call *or* we should be calling
you would call *or* you would be calling
they would call *or* they would be calling

PERFECT:
I have called *or* I have been calling
you have called *or* you have been calling
he has called *or* he has been calling
we have called *or* we have been calling
you have called *or* you have been calling
they have called *or* they have been calling

PLUPERFECT:
I had called *or* I had been calling, etc.

FUTURE PERFECT:
I shall have called *or* I shall have been calling, etc.

CONDITIONAL PERFECT:
I should have called *or* I should have been calling, etc.

IMPERATIVE: call (you); let/him/us/them call